D0098315

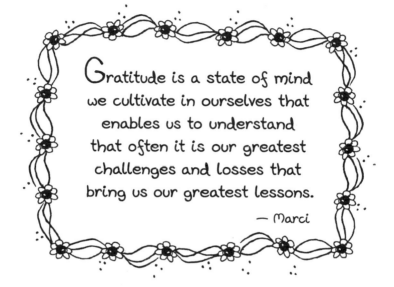

Gratitude is a state of mind
we cultivate in ourselves that
enables us to understand
that often it is our greatest
challenges and losses that
bring us our greatest lessons.

— Marci

ISBN: 978-1-68088-256-8

Children of the Inner Light is a registered trademark. Used under license.

▌ and Blue Mountain Press are registered in U.S. Patent and Trademark Office. Certain trademarks are used under license.

Printed in China.
First Printing: 2018

♻ This book is printed on recycled paper.

This book is printed on paper that has been specially produced to be acid free (neutral pH) and contains no groundwood or unbleached pulp. It conforms with the requirements of the American National Standards Institute, Inc., so as to ensure that this book will last and be enjoyed by future generations.

Blue Mountain Arts, Inc.
P.O. Box 4549, Boulder, Colorado 80306

The Power of Gratitude

Change Your Mind, Change Your Life

Marci

Blue Mountain Press™

Boulder, Colorado

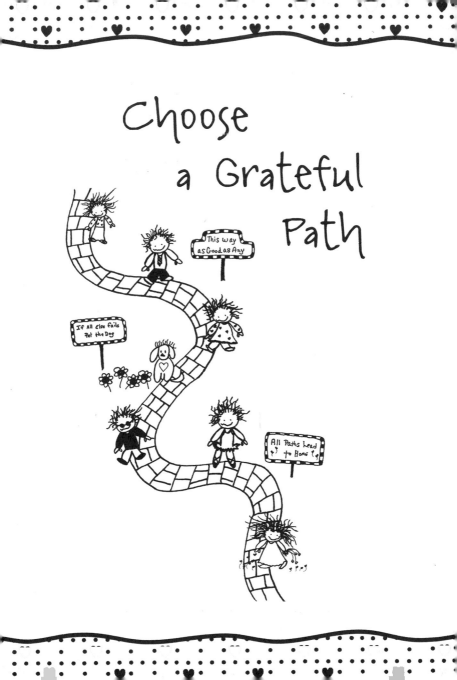

Gratitude is a state of thankfulness. Its deeper meaning is something we learn about all through our lives. When we are young, we are taught to say "thank you" when someone gives us something. But life has other lessons to teach us, because our spiritual growth is a priority for the universe. Its goal is that we become more —
more loving...
more giving...
more accepting...
more compassionate.
As we cultivate the state of mind that enables us to realize it is our greatest challenges and losses that bring us our greatest lessons, we begin to understand the gifts that are ours to share as we harness the power of gratitude.

Change Your Thoughts, Change Your Life

In a world with so much uncertainty and stress, feelings of gratefulness don't always come easily. Our lives can feel out of our control as we deal with illness, loss of loved ones, or financial strain. Instead of feeling thankful, we can be left wondering why life is so hard.

We can begin to regain our sense of balance by remembering that there *is* something we have control of, and that is what we feed our minds. We can make a decision to read inspirational material every day. We can practice saying "no" to negative thoughts. We can focus on what we *do* have instead of what is missing in our lives.

With resolve and effort, we will soon see that small actions and a change in thinking can make a big difference in the way we experience life.

I am loved.
I am happy.
I am home.

Positive Thinking Leads the Way

It is not always easy to be positive in today's world. Life is difficult... this is a basic fact. But we can make a change within ourselves to help encourage our feelings of thankfulness. This change takes a commitment and, just like all things that are worthwhile, requires work and time to feel the results. When we decide to be positive, we make a small change that can affect not just ourselves but also those around us. Will this alter life itself? Not really... but it will change *your* life and the way you feel as you meet the challenges of day-to-day living.

Give Thanks
for Each
Day in
Advance

Give thanks for the many blessings in store for you today... Give thanks for the things you clearly see as blessings and for those things not yet perceived as so. Keep in mind that God is always there for you, directing your path and often putting obstacles in your way that push you to take that other fork in the road. Open your heart to abundant grace. Ask that kindness be in your heart always. Let the compassion you feel for others grow as you give thanks for this day and for those to come.

Cultivate a
Grateful
Heart in
Difficult
Times

When you cannot change your situation because the things affecting you are beyond your control or the timing is not right for action, cultivate gratitude by doing these things:

Light a candle to remind you throughout the day that an angel is always watching over you.

Make a decision to find the good in every situation.

Start a gratitude list, and add something to it each day.

Reach out with understanding and hope to someone in need. Sharing gratitude always returns to renew the spirit.

Attitude Is Everything

If you have a negative attitude — when you open the door, that is what you'll find.

When we make a decision to maintain a positive attitude, something very significant happens inside of us. Even though our situation may not change, the way we feel in our day-to-day living does change for the better. And when we focus on what we can do, instead of on our shortcomings, we are more inclined to find solutions to our problems. When we develop an attitude of gratefulness for all the good things that are in our lives and let go of things not meant for us, we don't waste precious time and energy and we find we are more likely to see the path opening for us.

Look for the Positive, and You Will Find It

Most of the things in life we have no control over — but we do have a choice about how we see them.

Why do some people see things in a positive light and others in a negative? It's habit. Habits can be changed or developed with focused attention.

Just as an athlete trains his body to perform, one can train the mind toward healthy thinking.

Longtime patterns of thinking require work to effect change... make a decision and work at it every day.

When negative thoughts appear, say to yourself, "Don't go there."

Give Thanks
for New
Beginnings

Sometimes our lives take a turn that we never expected, and we are faced with a challenge to begin anew. We can feel overwhelmed and wonder if we can get through this day, much less the days ahead. Remember to take it one day at a time, accepting each day with courage and faith. Soon you may discover that a new beginning has opened a door you never imagined and shown you another path to take you home.

Acceptance Creates the Fertile Soil for Change

There are times in our lives when happiness seems to elude us. We want more... We wish we were further along in our lives... We desire better relationships... We try to push ourselves beyond where we are at the moment. Sometimes, all that is needed is a change of mind... a change called "acceptance." With this change there comes a sense of peace and a sudden realization that a shift in thinking has brought us the very things we were looking for all along!

Fighting against the way things are causes most personal suffering — acceptance is the path to serenity.

Accept that we each learn life's lessons in our own way.

FAITH
♥
HOPE
♥
LOVE
♥

Believe that ultimately everything happens for a reason. Acceptance leads the way to happiness.

Give Thanks for Your Family...

Our families give us the very first people to love us. They give us mentors to show us the way. They give us a mirror to hold up to see our best selves as we share wisdom, strength, and love. They see our best and worst and love us anyway. Some families we are born into... some families we are chosen by. Hug your family, and thank them for who they are.

...and for Your Friends

Friends are among our greatest treasures as we travel the road of life... walking beside us when we need comfort, standing behind us when we need support, and walking in front of us when we need to be shown the way.

Friends are there to hold our hands, to share our triumphs, and to shine a light of hope when the road gets dark. They bring so much to our lives. Friends remind us that some things do last forever, and friendship is one of them.

Give Thanks for Love

Love is much more than a feeling. Love is an action. It is the way you show love each day. It is a gentle touch, a loving embrace, and doing thoughtful things. It is sharing together the good times and working through the tough times.

Accept the love of others as they can give it — this is the way to experience unconditional love.

Focus only on the positive qualities of those you love — express gratitude.

To love and be loved... that is life's greatest gift. To share joy with those most important in our lives... that is a blessing.

Gratitude allows you to experience all the love in your life.

Love is the greatest gift of all.

Be Someone
Others
Will Be
Grateful
For

Be a powerful example of love in the world... live your beliefs.

Be compassionate. Life is difficult, and people are often working through private battles.

Be kind. Little ones are watching you and learning about compassion.

Be an encourager. The words "everything will be okay" can lighten the heart of another. Share love... there is an unending supply.

Be hopeful. Your attitude will uplift the spirit of another.

Be you. Let your light shine.

A
Thankful Heart
Is a
Gift to
Others

Love

Love grows on
seeds of Kindness.

Sometimes the most beautiful blessing is the one we bestow on another. Our attitudes are contagious, and when we take on a sunny disposition, those around us can't help but feel better too. When we offer an outstretched hand to someone who is hurting... encouragement to someone who is afraid... or give thanks to someone for their kindness... we receive the special gift of a grateful heart.

Counting Blessings
Is a
Gift to
Ourselves

When we remember to be grateful for the good things in our lives and express gratitude at the beginning of each day, we demonstrate a belief that all our needs are taken care of.

When we remain positive and hopeful about each new day, we change the way we feel and put loving energy into the world.

When we count our blessings, we give ourselves a beautiful gift called gratitude.

Gratitude Grows with Time

When we are young, we think the years don't pass quickly enough and we can't wait to be one year older. Then, suddenly, we are older! When we look back and wonder where the time has gone, we realize the road behind us is full of gifts that have made us rich. There's hard-earned wisdom... an appreciation for others... trials that made us stronger... hope given to others... prayers answered... love given and received... and we realize how truly blessed we are.

Turn around and look at your life — you will see that everything that has happened to you has put you where you are today.

Focus on the good things in life, and let go of the things not meant to be.

Express gratitude each day for what you have, who you are, and who you have been.

Happiness
Is Realizing
That the Best
Things
in
Life Are
Free!

We often look at successful people and expect them to be happy because they have "everything that money can buy." But if we speak to the wise or elderly, they tell us that life has taught them an important truth: Real treasures are not found in a chest of gold or even in a dream at the end of a rainbow. They are captured in those tiny, special moments that live in our hearts. These moments are created by the simple things: a walk... a talk... a laugh. They allow us to experience the priceless things: wisdom... hope... and love. Finally, we realize that *these* are the gems that are ours to keep forever, and we acknowledge our good fortune and say, "We have everything that money *can't* buy."

The Power of Gratitude

Gratitude is one of life's greatest gifts, and it is free for the choosing. When we make this choice, we are demonstrating an understanding of our free will.

Gratitude is a practice... an exercise in which we train our minds to look at the good things before us each day, no matter what is happening in our lives.

Gratitude is a state of mind we cultivate in ourselves that enables us to understand that the obstacles we've faced and the losses we've sustained have been our best teachers.

Gratitude is the place from which we recognize life's compensations that are always before us, so we can enjoy each day with thanksgiving.

Give Thanks
at the
End of
the Day

As you look back at the road you've traveled, remember to give thanks for these precious things: For the gift of family, either given or chosen... For the blessing of friendship and the joy that comes through sharing... For your growing understanding of our oneness as children of God... For your ability to see goodness in all things as you accept your losses with grace... For the hope that stays in your heart in every situation... For the gift of acceptance as you acknowledge that obstacles seemingly in the way of your path forward may be redirecting you toward a better plan... For the gift of faith because it is the foundation of every decision you make and for the many blessings not yet received.

About Marci

Marci began her career by hand painting floral designs on clothing. No one was more surprised than she was when one day, in a single burst of inspiration and a completely new and different art style, her delightful characters sprang from her pen! "Their wild and crazy hair is a sign of strength," she thought, "and their crooked little smiles are endearing." She quickly identified the charming characters as Mother, Daughter, Sister, Father, Son, Friend, and so on until all the people and places in life were filled. Then, with her own loved ones in mind, she wrote a true and special sentiment to each one. This would be the beginning of a wonderful success story, which today still finds Marci writing each and every one of her verses in this same personal way.

Marci is a self-taught artist who has always enjoyed writing and art. She is thrilled to see how her delightful characters and universal messages of love have touched the hearts and lives of people everywhere. Her distinctive designs can also be found on Blue Mountain Arts greeting cards, calendars, bookmarks, and other gift items.

To learn more about Marci, look for Children of the Inner Light on Facebook or visit her website: www.MARCIonline.com.